I0788912

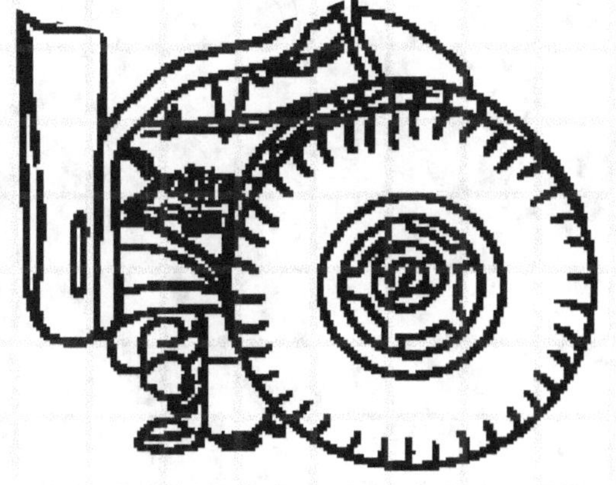

The U.S. consumes about half of the world's gasoline.

The longest tandem bicycle seated 35 people, it was more than 20 meters long.

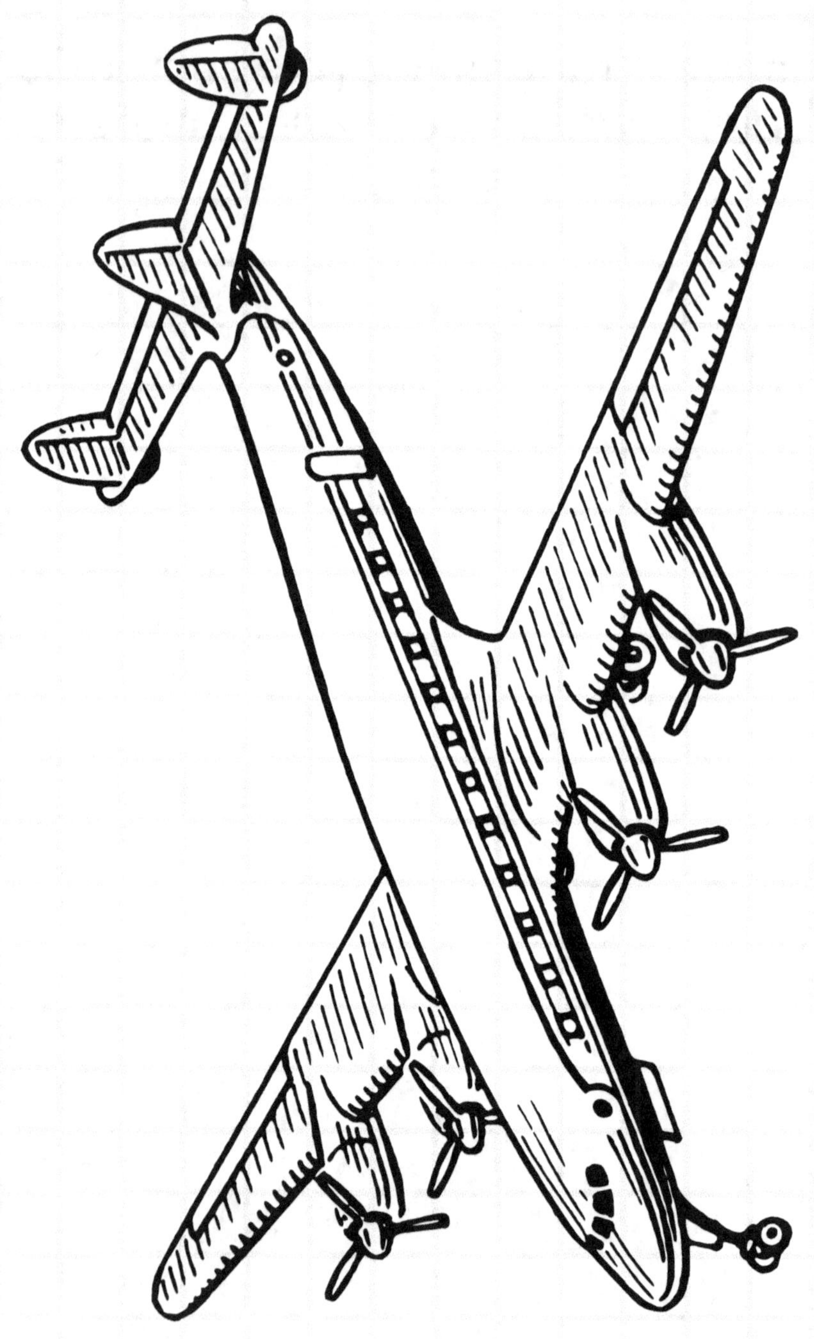

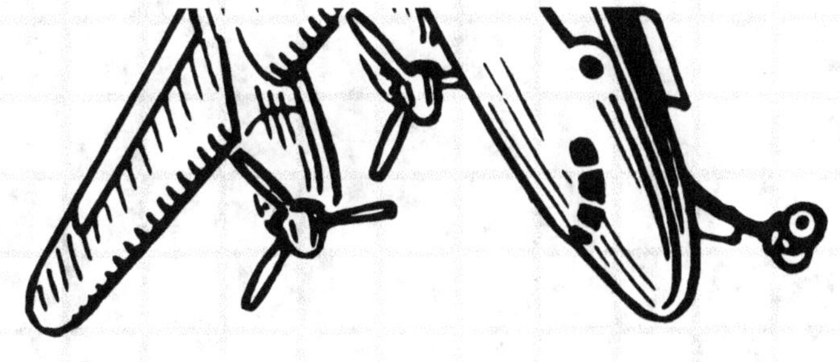

Some planes can fly for more than five hours after one of their engines goes out

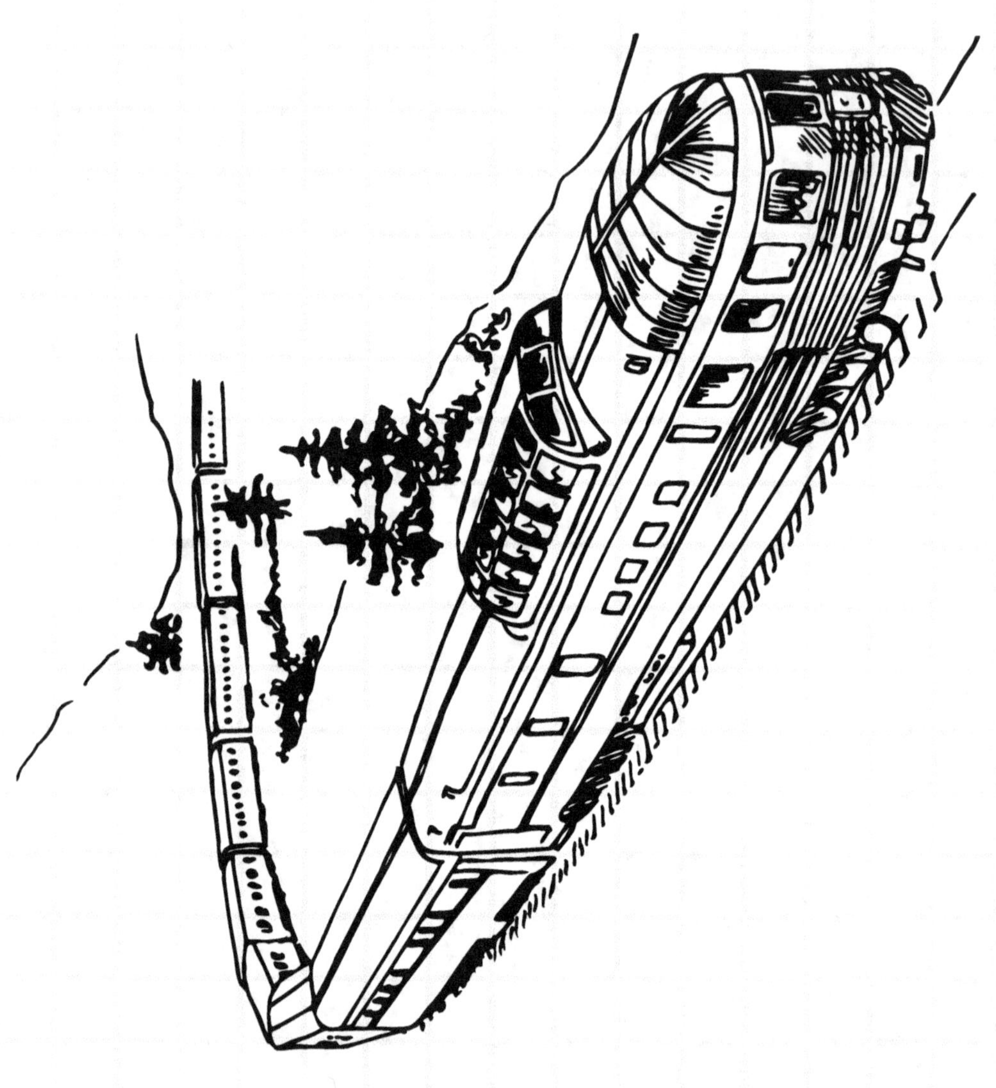

Some trains have a second locomotive which pushes the train forward from the back.

The difference between a boat and a ship lies in its weight. If a vessel is over 500 tones then it is called a ship. A ship can also carry a boat.

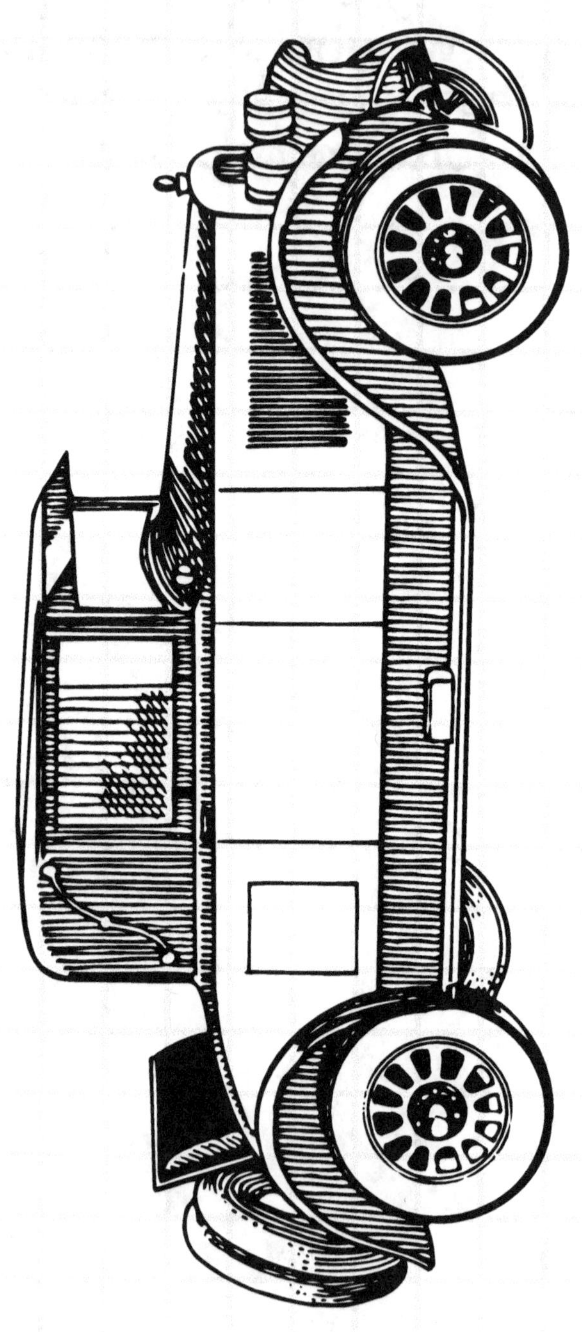

Traffic congestion wastes three billion gallons of gas each year.

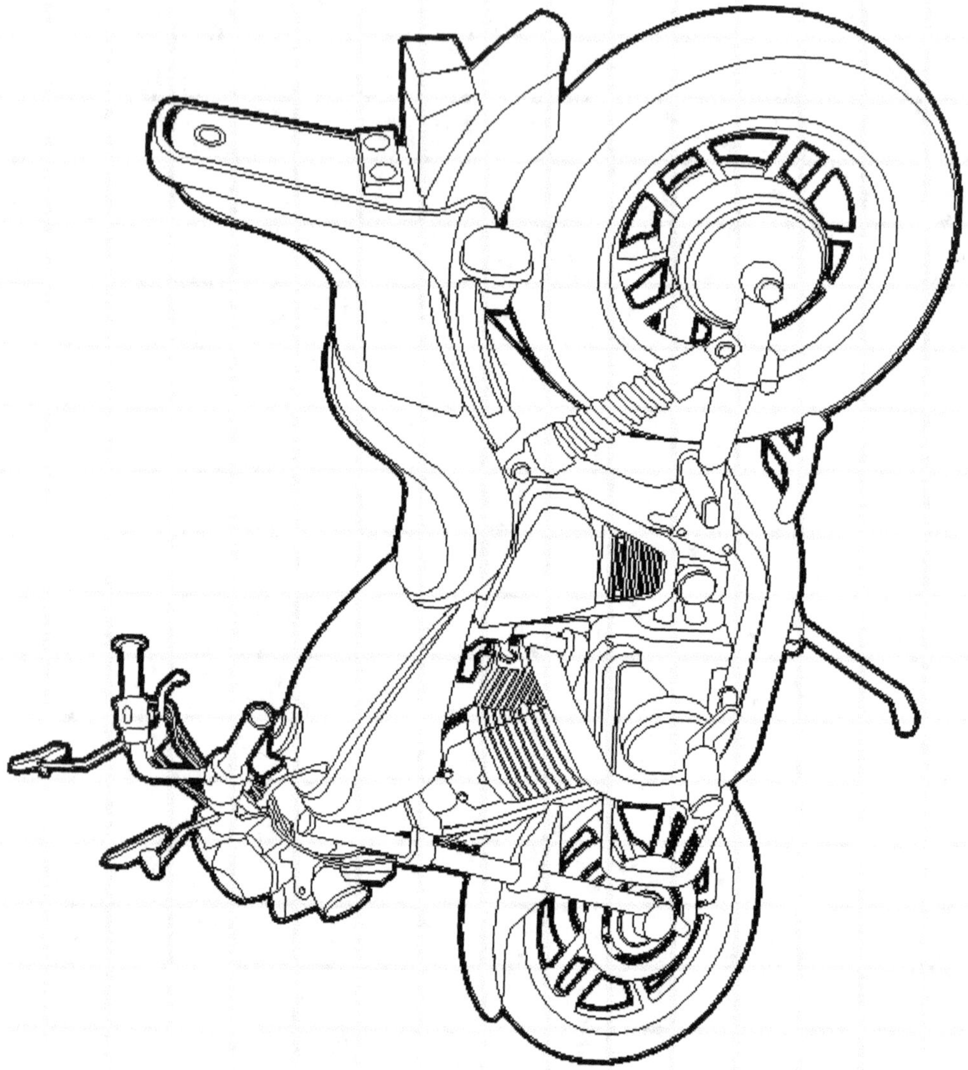

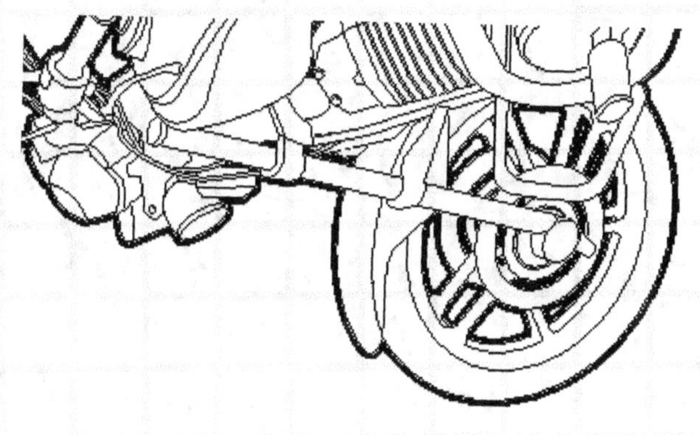

The world's most expensive bike costs $360,000

USAF

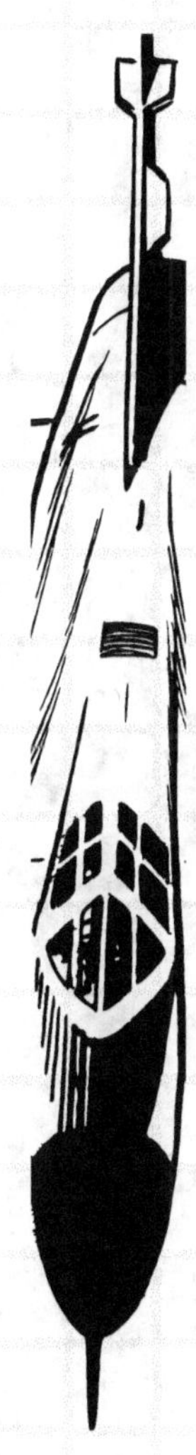

Current world record for the fastest manned aircraft. Its maximum speed was 7,200 km/h

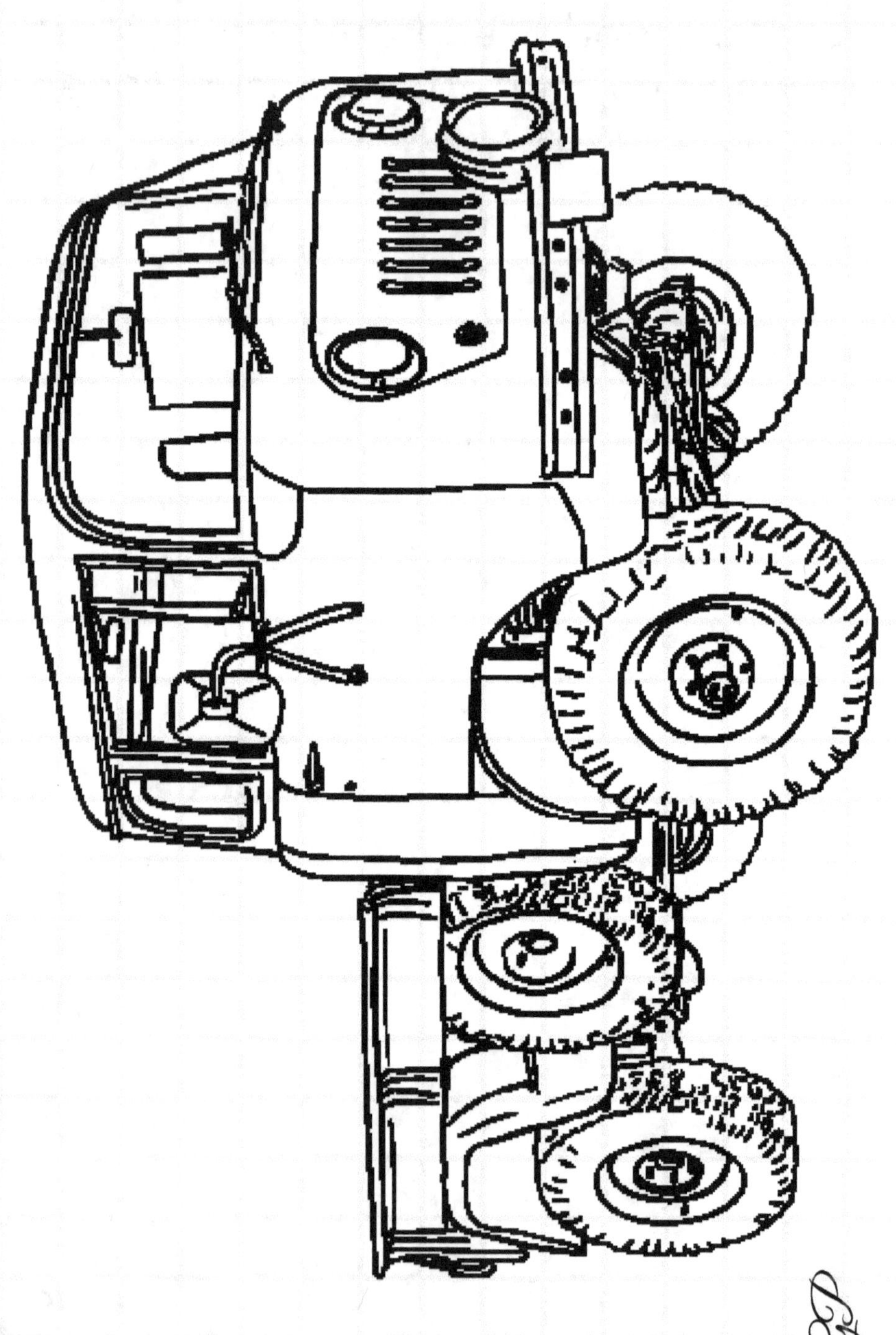

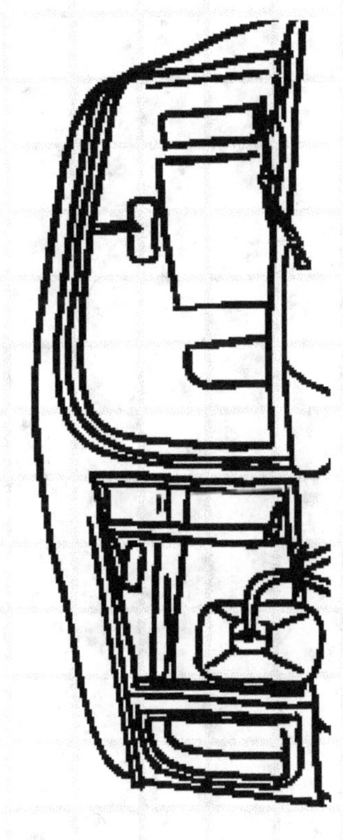

90 percent of drivers admit to signing
behind the wheel.

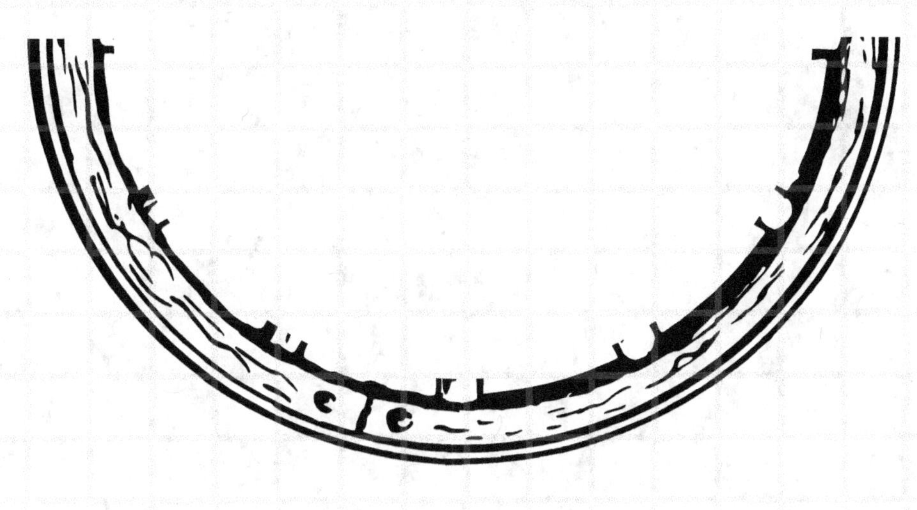

The first cars did not have steering wheels. They were operated by a lever.

The world manufactures about 100 million bikes each year

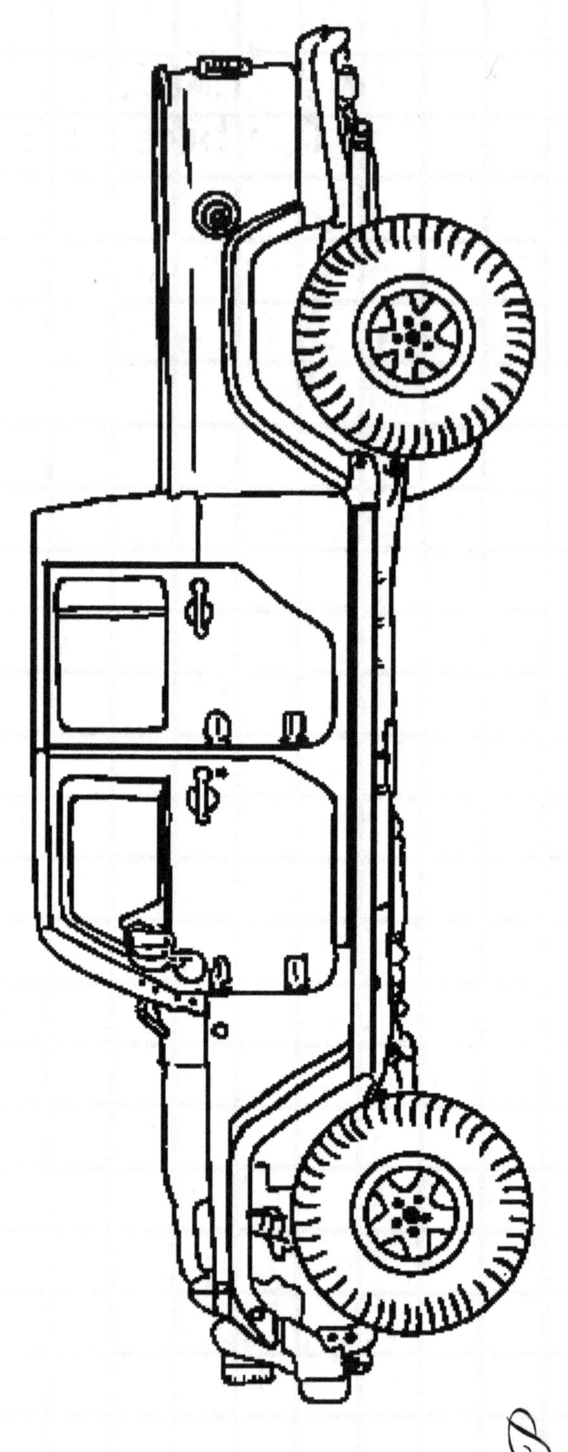

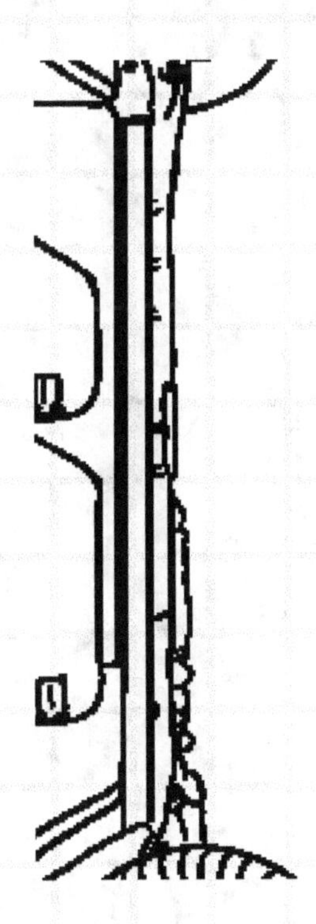

The average American will spend two weeks of his or her life stopped at red lights.

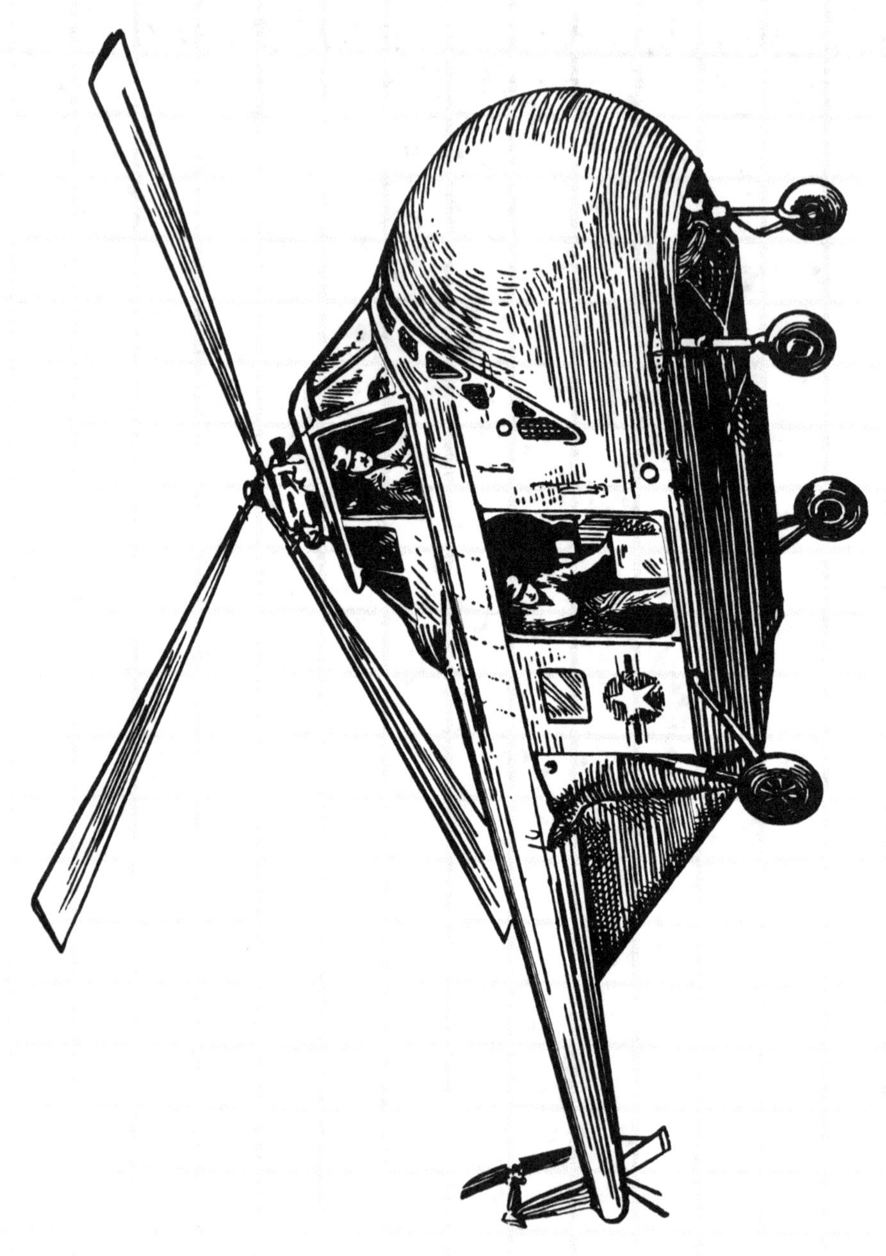

New models of helicopters are still being developed. Recently, the Eurocopter X3 hit a major milestone by reaching a speed of 293 mph.

The largest aerostat is 243 feet long

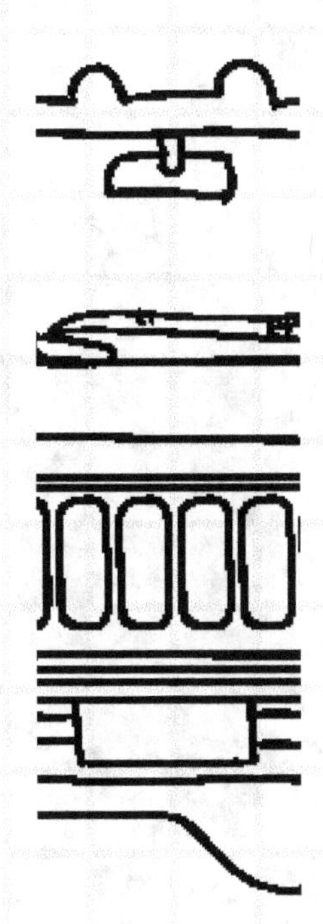

The most popular car color is white.

Most people think that the word helicopter is broken up by syllables. However, it is actually made up of two parts that are "helico," which means spiral, and "pter," which means made with wings.

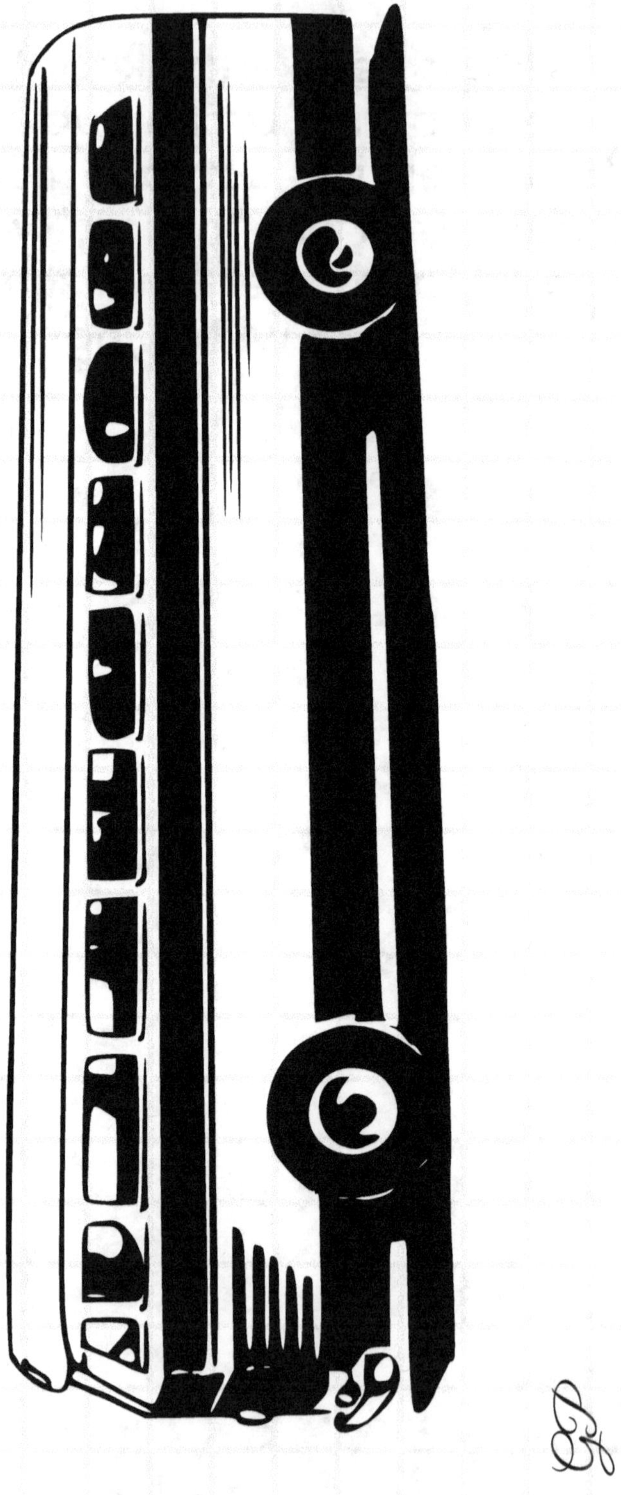

In 1900, Americans owned 8,000 cars, in 1920, they owned 8 million, and in the year 2000, there were more than 220 million.

The average consumer spends $400 a year on diagnostics, scheduled maintenance, and tune-ups.

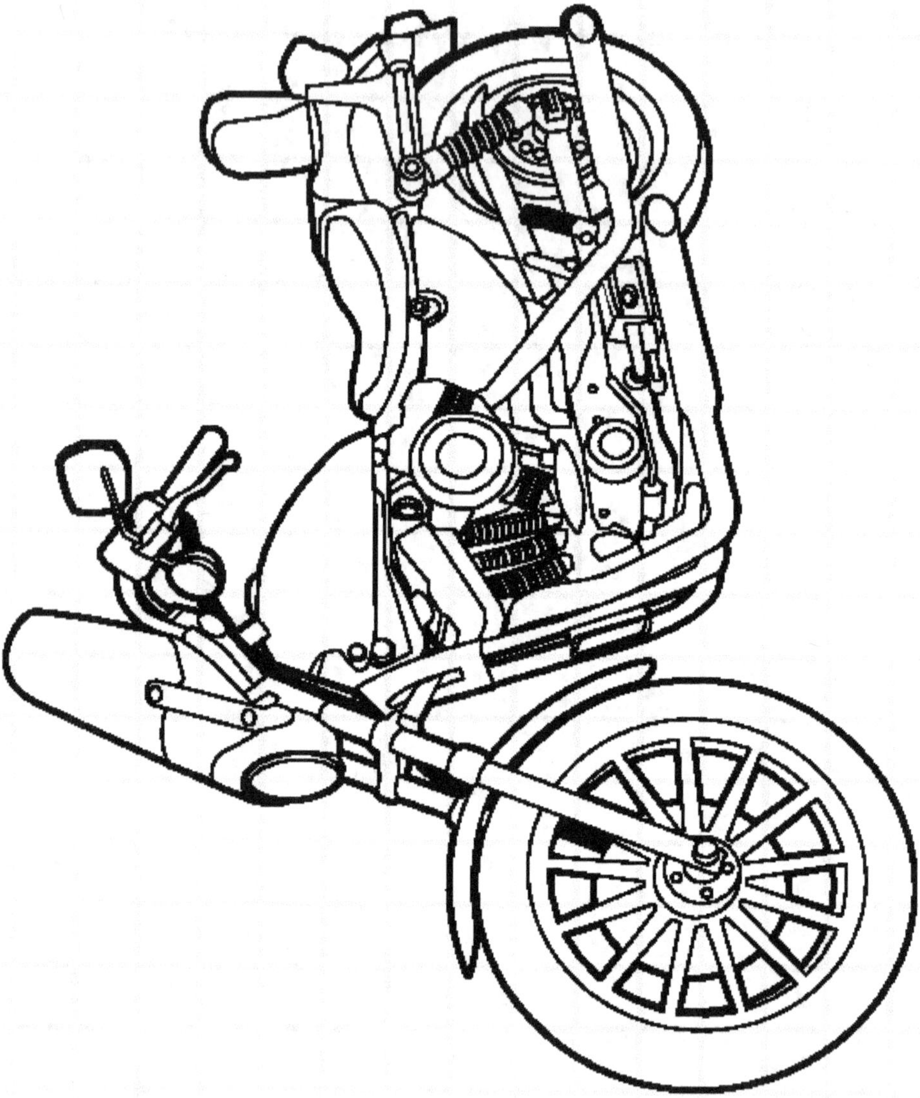

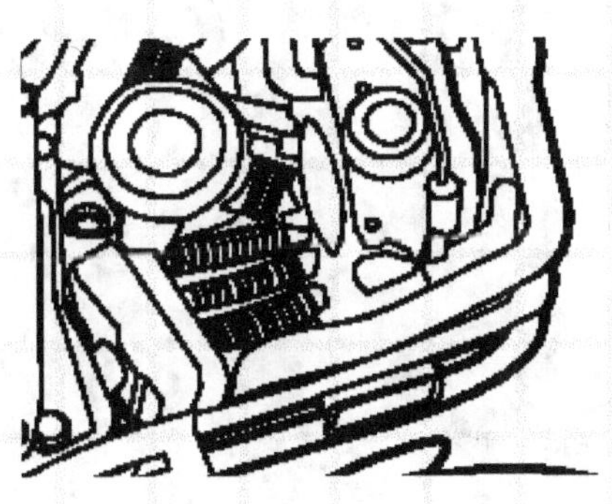

It is legal in California to drive a motorcycle between two cars in their lane (lane splitting) and only 53% of state residents know that it is legal.

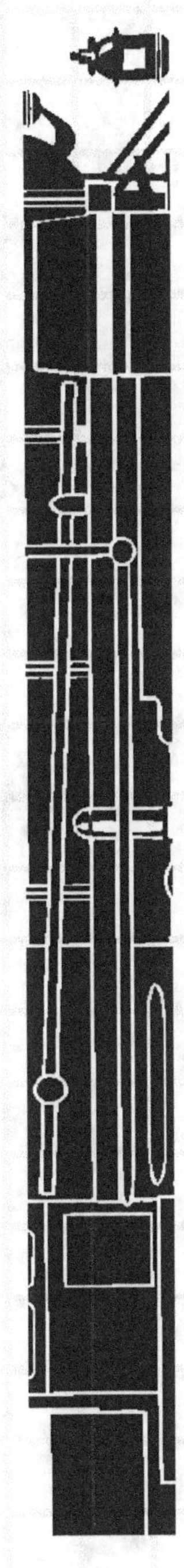

The first American locomotive lost to a horse.

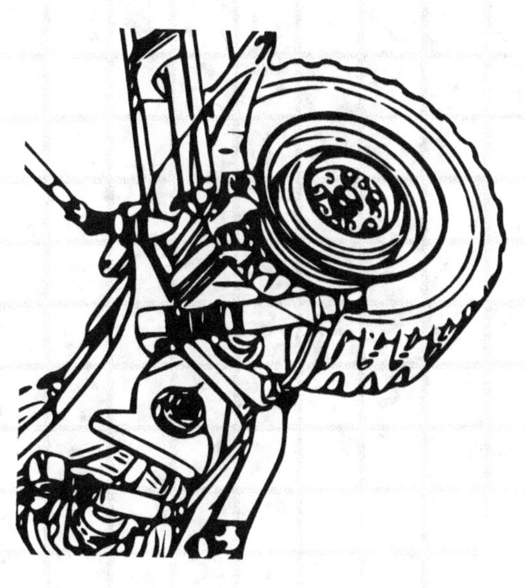

60 million cars are produced every year

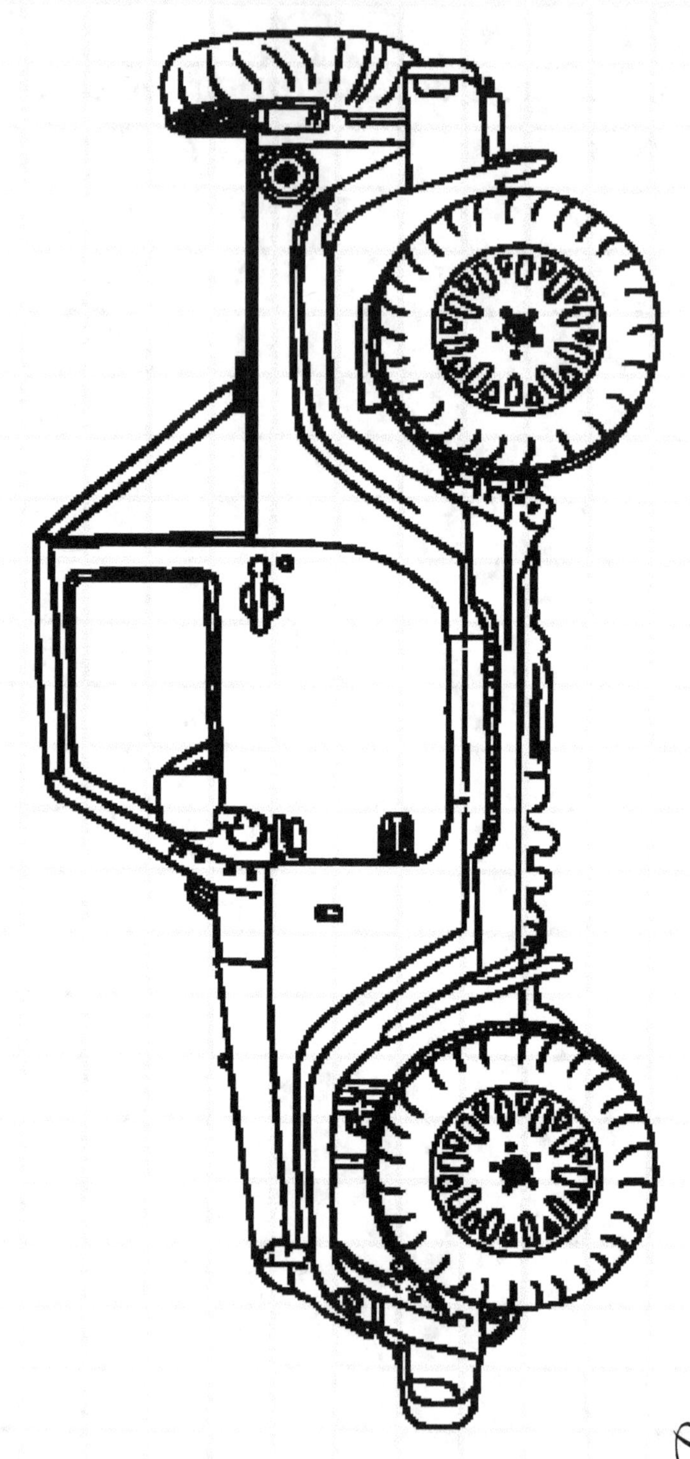

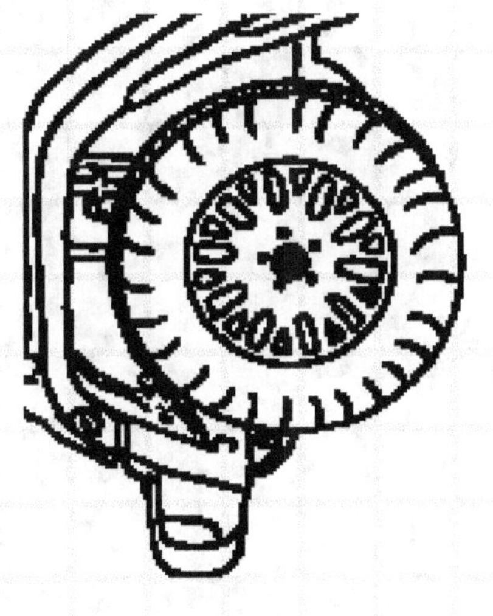

It would take less than a month to get
to the moon by car

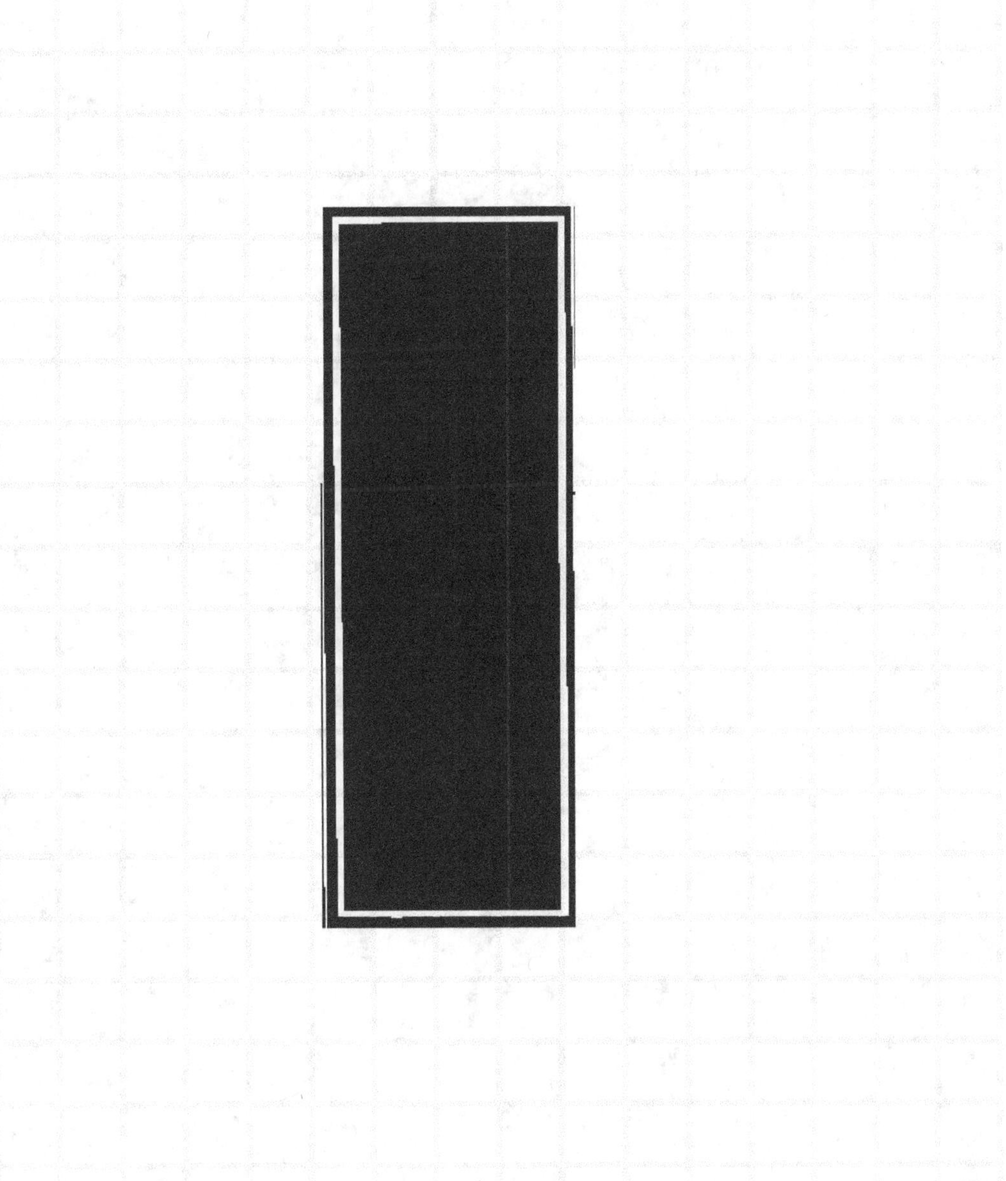

The magnetic-levitation train is currently the fastest train in the world.

Everybody's doing the locomotion . . . really. We are all engines, which by their most basic definition are machines that convert energy into motion.

SHARE YOUR DRAWINGS

Comment,rate and share the product so that I can continue to create

FB: Galas Products

Pinterest: https://pl.pinterest.com/GalasProducts

Instagram: Galasproducts

Twitter: @GalasProducts